PB AND J

TWO FRIENDS IN A JAM!

words and pictures
by Gio Velino

Hardcover: 978-1-7358578-0-0
Paperback: 978-1-7358578-1-7

Library of Congress Control Number: 2020918649

First edition, July 2021

Art, Text, Editing and Layout by Gio Velino

Printed by KDP and IngramSpark in the USA

www.bygiovelino.com

in memory of
Jerry and Lillian Pisano

Inside the fridge, right next to a tray,

sit the closest of friends: PB and J.

Together they're better than cheese and sliced meat,

a true lunchtime classic that cannot be beat.

You may be surprised, that once long ago,

these closest of friends were each other's worst foe.

Yes, things then were not at all sweet for these two.

I know the tale well – let me tell it to you.

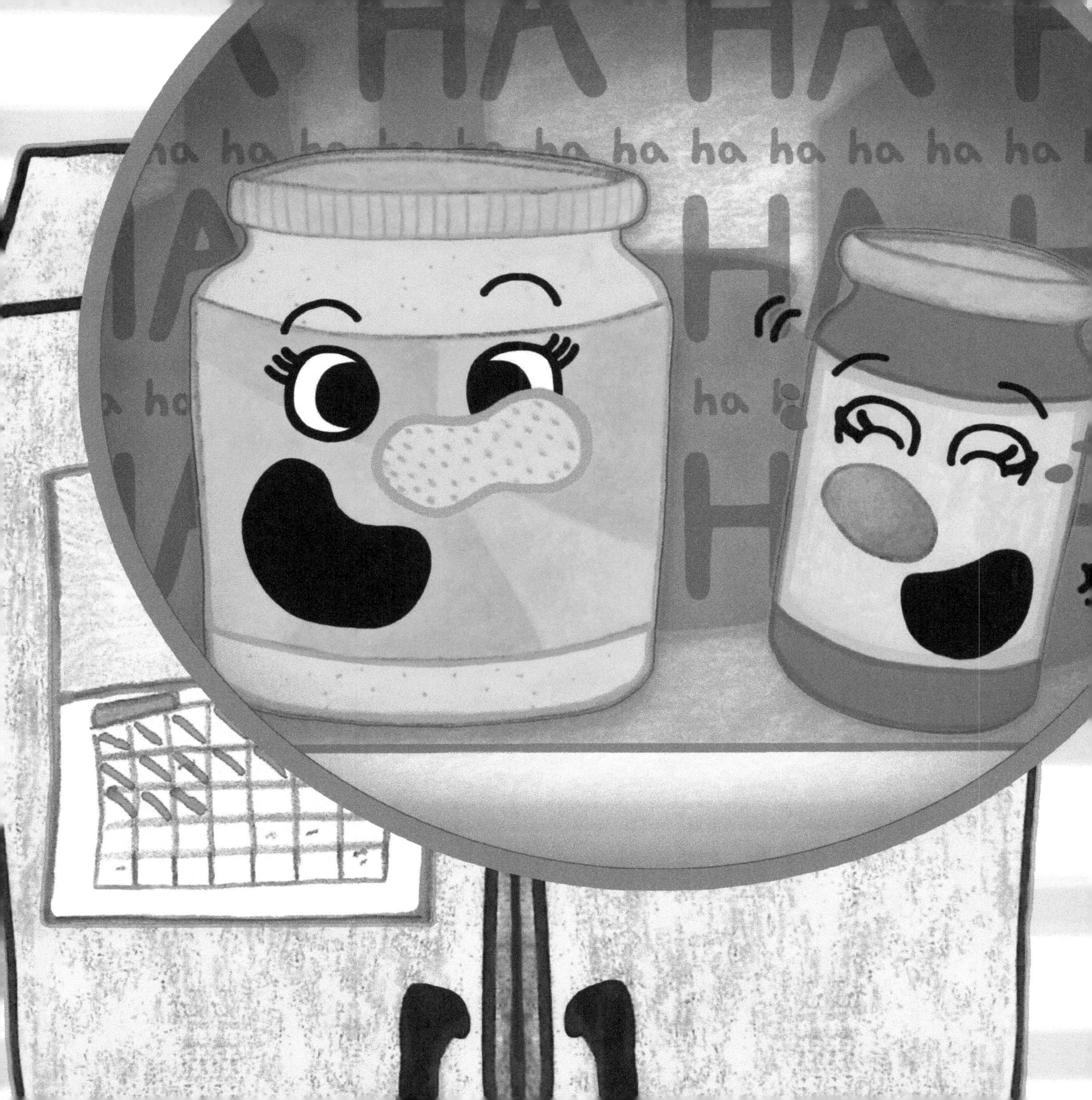
HA HA
ha ha ha ha ha ha ha

It began on a day just like any other,
when, groceries in hand, came home a proud mother.

She had purchased her usual veggies and fruit,
apples, bananas, and pears were her loot.

Preparing a sandwich for her child with care,
she heard when he called from the living room chair.

He said, "Mommy, may I please have some punch?"
"Sure," she replied, "It will go great with lunch!"

So she took out a lemon from her green grocery sack,

unaware that her kitchen was now under attack.

Lemon eyed PB and J with pain in her heart —
for she had no friends, and was thought of as tart.

And as Apple, Banana, and Pear joined the two
she watched from afar, and her sourness grew.

Quickly, Lemon thought up a scam —
she'd make herself friends by creating a jam!

So as mom grabbed a spoon to make punch on the double,
Lemon snuck away to go stir up some trouble.

Creeping over to J while no one was near,

Lemon softly whispered her lies in her ear:

"Did you know PB told me she thinks that you're gross?

Why, she says that you're not even tasty on toast!"

J gasped – for this news really shocked her!

She never thought that sweet PB would mock her.

But since it was spoken, J thought it was true,
and she felt there was only one thing she could do:

"Lemon, tell PB if she thinks I'm icky,
then she should know I think that she is too sticky!"

"Whatever you say," Lemon said with a grin.
Now her sour scheme was about to begin!

As soon as poor J was far out of her sight,
Lemon found others to further the fight.

"Hey guys, guess what?" she said, batting her lashes,
"J says PB made her break out in rashes!"

"What?!" cried Banana, "That cannot be so!
They're the closest of friends, all three of us know."

"I bet it's PB's fault!" Pear exclaimed,
but Apple said no, it was J that he blamed.

Lemon sat back, having done her bad deed,

to watch trouble unfold – she had planted her seed.

Pear joined J once she was able,

while PB and Apple jumped up on the table.

"I swear to Carver!" PB said with a huff,

"I refuse to share bread with that soggy stuff!"

"Oh yeah?" J stuttered and shouted right back,

"You're nuts if you think that you're a good snack!

I'll have you know you're a jar of gross goo,

it's me who would hate to get stuck next to you!"

Banana stood by, unsure where to start –
when her friends were at odds it just peeled her apart.

Whispering to Banana, Lemon grinned wide,
"It looks like you need to go pick a side!"

How Banana wanted to speak out and split up the fight!
She knew taking sides between friends wasn't right.

Just then she saw a knife passing through –
maybe, just maybe, he'd know what to do!

So she called him on over to help out her friends,
hoping that soon they could all make amends.

"I hate to cut in," Knife said with a frown,
"but mind if I ask why ~~you~~ you're all feeling down?"

J was the first to break down and exclaim,
"Lemon said PB thinks that I'm lame!"

"I never said that!" PB gasped as she spoke,
"What is all this, some kind of sick joke?"

Lemon told ME that J thinks I'm unfair,
and is allergic to me now from out of thin air!"

"Hold on," said Knife, sharp as can be –
"Perhaps Lemon went on a gossiping spree!"

All eyes turned to Lemon who turned a deep pink,
"I can explain guys, it's not what you think..."

Then her voice shrank as she choked on her lie —
her eyes filled with tears, and she started to cry!

How Lemon sobbed as she stammered with shame,
"I'm so sorry guys, I know I'm to blame.

All I wanted was to talk with you guys —
I know it was wrong of me to start lies."

"Sorry, J!" PB said, "We shouldn't have fought.
I'm mad at Lemon now that she's caught."

"Hey now," said Knife, giving PB a nudge.
"Lemon said sorry– let's not hold a grudge."

"Okay, we'll forgive her," PB and J both agreed,
"We're friends again, and that's all that we need."

Banana then cheered and cried with delight,
"Thank you, good Knife, for ending this fight!"

She asked their new friends if they'd all like to stay,
as they came from a drawer that was far and away.

Knife smiled and said, "Glad to come lend a hand!
But we've got to go, and spread peace through the land.

Now before we cut out, here's advice for your crew:
It's not wise to share things you're not sure are true.

And if you're unhappy don't say things unkind—
for rumors, once started, are hard to unwind."

Then Knife, Fork, and Spoon left as fast as they came,

but for these grateful friends things were never the same.

THE END!

CPSIA information can be obtained
at www.ICGtesting.com
Printed in the USA
BVHW022346240821
615133BV00005B/340